JOSH MACDONALD

The Ambassador Angle

**SUMMIT
AUTHORITY**
PRESS

First published by Summit Authority Press 2025

Library of Congress Control Number: 2025910492

First edition

ISBN: 979-8-9990005-0-7

This book was professionally typeset on Reedsy.
Find out more at reedsy.com

Dedicated to the memory of my grandfather, Dave MacDonald.

Contents

1

The Angle Is Everything

Most ads fail.

Not because the product sucks. Not because the audience is wrong. Not even because the platform is saturated. Most ads fail because they don't say anything worth hearing.

They're flat. Predictable. Designed by marketers who've never actually sold anything at scale. People who think a cool hoodie and 20% off is a campaign. It's not.

A campaign is an *angle*.

The angle is the hook that bypasses logic and goes straight for the brainstem. It's the reason someone clicks, converts, buys, and sends it to five friends. It's the difference between a mediocre 3x ROAS and your product flying off the shelf before you even hit publish on your next ad.

Every time we launched something big, it started with an angle. Not a brand. Not a product. An angle. The angle came before the product.

Some people call them hooks. In growth marketing circles, they're "growth hacks." But the word doesn't really matter. The angle is the hack. It's the secret move, the unfair advantage.

A great angle is how you create revenue before anyone knows your name.

And when the angle's good enough?

You don't need investors.

You don't need to burn cash.

You don't even need time.

We were profitable from day one.

Not in theory—in reality.

The ad ran, the sales came in, the margin was there. No magic. No loss-leading. Just a sharp idea, timed right, executed fast.

Believe it or not, that's still possible.

Most people just never find the angle.

It doesn't work for every industry. It's not always available. But when the stars line up—timing, demand, social dynamics, ad platform behavior—you can print money. Until everyone else copies it. And by the time they do, you're already gone.

This book is about one of those angles.

It wasn't a fluke. It wasn't genius. But it was smart. And fast. And timed perfectly.

We took an Instagram trend, reverse-engineered the psychology behind it, and sold it back to the market at scale. First with swimwear. Then with sunglasses. It worked because we didn't try to convince people our product was the best. We made them feel like they were becoming something.

We didn't sell swimsuits.

We sold significance.

We sold identity.

We sold belonging.

And the best part? We made them apply for it.

2

We Saw It First: The Sunny Co Spark

It started with a red swimsuit.

Not a face. Not a name. Just a brunette, sitting poolside in a red one-piece, legs in the water, hair down, back turned. You couldn't see her face—just that sunlit pose, framed perfectly for Instagram. There was a small white logo on the back of the suit, but no one cared. The image wasn't about branding—it was about urgency.

I saw it reposted by girls on my feed, again and again. Same photo. Same pose. All tagging @sunnycoclothing.

None of them were in the photo. But that didn't matter.

Sunny Co Clothing had launched a *free plus shipping* offer, aimed at a demographic that hadn't seen that model before. Or maybe they had, and just didn't care. It felt new. It felt like a deal.

Repost this photo. Get the suit free. Just cover shipping.

The *free+shipping* model is exactly what it sounds like. The customer pays nothing for the product, but they do pay for shipping—typically something like $9. Behind the scenes, the merchant might only pay $3 to ship at volume, and maybe $2 for the product itself. That leaves a $4 profit per order. It's basic—but it works, especially when the perceived value is high and the audience is unfamiliar with the trick.

Sunny Co hit the perfect storm. The product looked valuable. The offer sounded like a glitch in the system. And the image— this clean, face-hidden, universal red suit—spread on its own. No ad spend. No push. Just pure momentum.

Within 24 hours, they gained over 750,000 followers on Instagram. Their Shopify store buckled under the traffic. Reports varied—some claimed over 2,000 orders in a single day, while others said the campaign pulled in $290,000 in sales within 24 hours.

But the thing about virality is that it doesn't care if you're ready.

They weren't.

There was no cap on redemptions. No inventory plan. No clarity around fulfillment. Refunds poured in. Comment sections turned hostile. The entire campaign went from brilliant to broken in less than 48 hours.

I sent the post to Bryan.

We weren't business partners yet—just long-time online friends. We'd never met, but we chatted daily like I did with most marketers in my circle back then. Swapping ideas, breaking down launches, watching what moved.

He was in the U.S. I was still in school at the University of Toronto.

I didn't send it as a pitch.

I sent it as a spark.

Within minutes, he had names, schools, social profiles, and background details on the Sunny Co team. He didn't just Google—he investigated. Pulled threads until the whole thing unraveled.

And that's saying something.

I had a computer science background. I'd been writing code, launching software, and building online since before college—years ahead of anyone I ever met in real life. But Bryan? He put my abilities to shame.

He didn't just research—he *knew*. I have no idea what tools he used or where he looked, but somehow, he found everything. Stuff that didn't show up on Google. Stuff I didn't even think was public.

If it ever existed online—in a post, a record, a buried subdomain—he'd find it.

Turns out what they were doing wasn't hard. Just a couple college kids from Arizona. Still in school. No track record. No real campaign experience. Definitely no backup plan for what to do when 750,000 people hit refresh at the same time.

These guys were hobbyists. We were professionals.

Bryan had been in the trenches for years. He was older than me—late 20s—and I'd seen his screenshots: $10k days, affiliate dashboards, campaign breakdowns. But what stuck with me most was one photo he sent me: a binder, the kind kids used to use for baseball cards, except every sleeve held a credit card.

Rows and rows of cards. Hundreds. All tied to different business entities, used to push spend, scale campaigns, bypass limits. It was like looking at a surgeon's toolkit—except his operating room was inside the ad platforms themselves.

Nothing illegal. Just clever.

And in a space where most people break rules without understanding them, Bryan knew how to stretch the system without snapping it.

This was the guy I was about to build with.

So when he said,
"We can do this,"
he didn't mean *try*.
He meant *scale*.

We wouldn't use the same angle. We didn't want to offer "free." We didn't want to attract deal hunters. We wanted *control*. Our play would be clean, paid, engineered. No refund storms. No chaos.

But the concept was solid. The reaction was real.

And we knew how to weaponize that.

We did a little research. Turns out the guys behind Sunny Co were just some college kids in Arizona. Same age as us. Less experience. No hate—we respected the spark. But they didn't have the experience to handle what they'd built.

Bryan and I did.

I wasn't just juggling university classes—I was coasting through them. Doing what was necessary to pass, sure, but my real focus was the same as it had been for years: making serious money online.

By that point, I'd already been in digital marketing for nearly a decade. I started at 14. By 16, I was pulling in over $10,000 a month. I'd already sold a software company. I'd built a name for myself in certain circles—not through hype, but through execution. Some of the most successful marketers I knew were a decade or two older than me, but they treated me as a peer. Many had been my customers. Respect came naturally when the results were undeniable.

Bryan had even more experience. He was wired for performance. He understood traffic in a way few people did. Between the two of us, we knew how to build funnels, test angles, push spend, and make the numbers work.

We didn't need investors.

We didn't need a runway.

We didn't even need time.

All we needed was a name.

I opened a list of girl names and started reading them out loud.

"Chloe... Madison... Brielle."

"Yup," Bryan said. "That's the one."

Brielle Beach Co.

No story. No legacy.

Just a vibe.

And just like that, we were in the swimwear business.

3

Swimwear and Psychology

We didn't know what we were doing.

But we knew we could make money.

That's how Brielle Beach Co began.

We didn't have a product background. We didn't have fashion industry experience. But we did have instincts. We understood timing, attention, and distribution—and in 2017, that's all you needed. Facebook ads were still forgiving. Not easy, but not like today. CPMs were manageable. Creative mattered more than compliance. You could still win with brute force and a decent angle.

So we started the only way we knew how:

We ordered a boatload of swimsuits off Alibaba.

We didn't know what we were getting. We didn't even know which styles were trending, and we didn't pretend to. We knew what girls our age were posting on Instagram, but that didn't mean the style still had momentum. Fashion has a lag. What looks hot today might be 12 months old—and by the time you scale a product and ship inventory, you're already behind.

So we needed real-world feedback.

We hired func.media to help with the first photoshoot. They had connections with models—girls who actually matched our target demo—and that gave us something we couldn't fake: access to honest, in-market opinions. These weren't stylists or fashion insiders. These were the girls buying the suits.

We looked into renting venues.

The quotes came back: tens of thousands of dollars.

Not happening.

Bryan was funding the whole operation. And we had an agreement—he would bankroll the venture, and I wouldn't take a dollar until he made back his investment. That meant we kept it lean. No fluff. Every dollar had to go to the shot that moved us forward.

We found a hotel in Toronto with a rooftop pool—nothing extravagant, but clean lines, sharp views, and the CN Tower standing tall in the background like it was photobombing us on purpose. The kind of place you wouldn't think twice about on a weekday, but that morning it felt like we had the city to ourselves.

The only catch? They'd let us shoot there—if we booked a room.

Deal.

So we booked it. Call time was 10am. Models showed up, coffee in hand, ready to go.

Inside the room? Chaos.

A couple massive, beat-up cardboard boxes sat on the floor, still bruised from the shipment out of China. I'd cracked them open days earlier, and now they barely held together—split at the seams, spilling out bags of swimsuits. No hangers, no tags, no sorting. Just piles of product crammed together from the factory floor to our makeshift showroom.

The bed became our display table. By the time everything was laid out, there had to be fifty bikinis covering every inch of that duvet. It looked like a flash sale at sea level. The models loved it. They picked through the colors and cuts, held them up, swapped picks, and dove into try-ons like they were shopping for themselves. I don't know what func.media paid them—but at that point, they probably would've done it just for the free bikinis.

As they gave feedback—what fit, what didn't, what they liked—I was scribbling notes on the sheets of paper covered in meaningless SKUs, trying to keep up. It wasn't organized, but it worked.

BRIELLE BEACH CO

PHOTOSHOOT #1

ITEM #	SIZE	COLOUR	MODEL	FIT	QUALITY	STYLE	NOTES
LC41721XS	XS	BLACK					
LC41072-S	S	BLACK					
LC41455-S	S	BLACK					
LC410095-8S	S	BLUE					
LC41392S	S	PURPLE				SOLID	
LC41324-2S	S	BLACK					
LC410095-7S	S	FLUORESCENT YELLOW					
LC41487S	S	WHITE					
LC41681S	S	BLACK					
LC410150S	S	BLUE					
LC41272-2S	S	YELLOW/BLACK/BLUE					
LC410138S	S	BLACK/WHITE STRIPED					
LC40467-2S	S	BLACK					
LC41455-M	M	BLACK					
LC41072-M	M	BLACK					
LC41658-2M	M	BLACK					
LC41654-1M	M	WHITE					
LC41825-M	M	BLACK/WHITE					
LC41272-2M	M	YELLOW/BLACK/BLUE					
LC41279-2L	L	BLACK					
LC42132-16	ONE	CREAM					
SK001	S	BLACK					
SK002	M	RED					
SK003	L	WHITE					
SK004	S	WHITE					
SK005	S	YELLOW					
SK006	S	ORANGE					
SK007	S	BLACK					
SK008	S	PINK					
SK009	S	TURQUOISE					

One page of SKUs I would have wrote notes on.

One by one, they changed and stepped out to the rooftop.

The pool sparkled. The tower loomed.

Toronto delivered—and we got exactly what we came for.

The only person missing? Bryan.

He wasn't there. He was the one funding the whole operation, and yet somehow he missed the best part—a rooftop shoot in the middle of summer with models, drinks, and the city skyline behind us.

We sent him photos, gave him the play-by-play. But it wasn't the same.

He was financing bikinis.

We were hanging poolside.

Poor guy.

It was a little early in the day for a drink—but what else were we going to do? Waste a perfect rooftop morning? We had the hotel. We had the crew. We had models in bikinis and a full spread of inventory. It felt less like a photoshoot and more like the kind of day people pretend to live on Instagram.

So we ordered drinks.

And the photos?

They turned out great. Clean, candid, scroll-stopping.

No overproduction. No fake filters.

Just real light, real people, and a product that was about to become a business.

We started using the photos immediately—to build landing pages, run ads, and most importantly, to set the foundation for what would later become the ambassador angle.

At first, it was simple. We tried recruiting ambassadors to kickstart an influencer campaign. We messaged girls offering free swimwear in exchange for a little promotion. It wasn't some masterstroke—it was just a common way to get traction.

But the response was overwhelming.

Way more interest than we expected.

Almost every girl wanted in.

And that's when it clicked.

We didn't need to give the swimsuits away.

We could charge for them.

Because we weren't just selling swimsuits anymore.

We were selling *association*.

Instagram had trained a generation to chase social currency— and we were handing it out.

Everyone wanted to be an ambassador—even more than they wanted the free swimsuits.

So we let them.

No application. No vetting.

Just buy the swimsuit, and you're in.

No barrier. No mystery.

Just a dopamine hit wrapped in a discount code.

We'd found our angle.

And this time—it was ours.

4

Built to Sell, Not to Wear

At first, we thought we needed influencers.

That was the plan: message a few girls, give them a discount, maybe some free product, and get them to post in exchange. We figured it'd help us get early traction—classic startup stuff.

But what happened next changed everything.

The response was overwhelming.

Not just yeses—*enthusiastic* yeses.

Girls weren't hesitating. They *wanted* to be ambassadors.

It wasn't just about getting a free bikini. It was about what it meant to *have a brand choose you*. The Instagram generation had been trained to see their identity as a highlight reel. And now we were giving them a new badge to post.

They weren't just wearing the product.

They were *being seen* in it.

And more importantly—they were being *labeled* as something.

We didn't need to chase influencers.

We needed to reverse the funnel.

Instead of picking people and hoping they posted, we let the masses come to us.

We built a funnel that made everyone feel special.

Step 1: See the ad.

Step 2: Apply to become an ambassador.

Step 3: Get "accepted" via email 30–60 minutes later.

Step 4: Activate your status with a 70% off code (a rate which we A/B tested constantly).

Step 5: Post it on social.

Suddenly, we weren't in the bikini business anymore.

We were in the identity business.

People weren't buying the suit. They were buying the status that came with it.

They wanted the title.

They wanted to be picked.

And the beauty of it?

They were picking *themselves*.

We didn't even need to fake scarcity.

We made the "acceptance" email feel like a big deal.

And the conversions poured in.

The economics worked from day one. We charged for shipping—more than it cost us. That alone covered most of the product cost, and the discount was structured to still give us a margin. We weren't bleeding cash. We weren't loss-leading. This wasn't a VC-backed fantasyland.

This was a money machine—with a better story than anyone else in the market.

We didn't invent the ambassador model.

But we packaged it in a way that felt *new*.

We made it scale.

Initially, we didn't have the best product.

But we had the best *angle*.

5

The Pivot: Abella Eyewear

Brielle worked.

But it was messy.

Swimwear had problems.

Sizing. Returns. Fit issues.

Every order came with a chance of disappointment. That's manageable when you're self-fulfilling a dozen orders a day— but a nightmare when you're scaling.

And then there was the top-and-bottom issue. I learned— honestly, for the first time—that you can't just pair a size small top with a small bottom and assume it works for everyone. Some girls wear a medium bottom and a small top. Or vice versa. Multiply that across styles, colors, and inventory? It turns into a logistics problem real quick.

On top of that, the sizing from Asia didn't match U.S. sizing.

Asian factories ran small—at least one full size down from what American customers expected.

So a "medium" in China? Often an "extra small" here.

That kind of mismatch kills trust.

Swimwear shoot in San Diego.

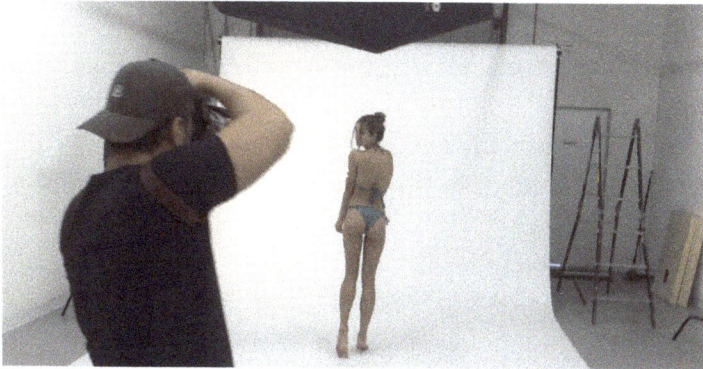

Once volume picked up, we had many more photo shoots.

It wasn't just a product problem—it was a brand problem. People associate sizing problems with low-quality Chinese factories.

We knew if we wanted real volume, we needed a simpler product.

No sizing.

No confusion.

Just something anyone could wear—and no one could mess up.

We landed on sunglasses.

The pivot wasn't glamorous. But it was fast.

It happened on a five-hour Skype call one night in February 2018. I was in Fort Myers, Florida, visiting family—working off a cramped writing desk in a spare bedroom. Bryan was in California. We usually messaged back and forth—Skype chat was our main operating system. But this time we called. There was too much to do, and we needed speed.

Video on. Head down.

We weren't brainstorming—we were building.

From scratch.

Within five hours, we went from nothing to a fully functional Shopify store.

Name. Domain. Branding. Products. Ads. Live.

The idea came somewhere around hour two.

Sunglasses.

Clean, scalable, no sizing, no returns.

Bryan leaned back in his chair, hit his vape, and gave that quick half-laugh he did whenever something clicked.

"Let's just do sunglasses," he said.

"No sizing. No returns. Just clean."

That was it. Simple call. Easy pivot.

And it made sense.

We finished the entire setup that night—Abella was live before we went to sleep.

The site was built. The products were listed.

All that was left was to let the ad system catch up.

No fanfare. No PR. No warm-up campaign.

Just some new creative, a product switch, and the same core funnel logic that built Brielle.

The next morning, the Facebook ads were approved.

Traffic started flowing. Conversions followed.

Revenue came in before we even had a chance to overthink anything.

First day?

It was somewhere between $600 and $800 in sales.

On almost no ad spend.

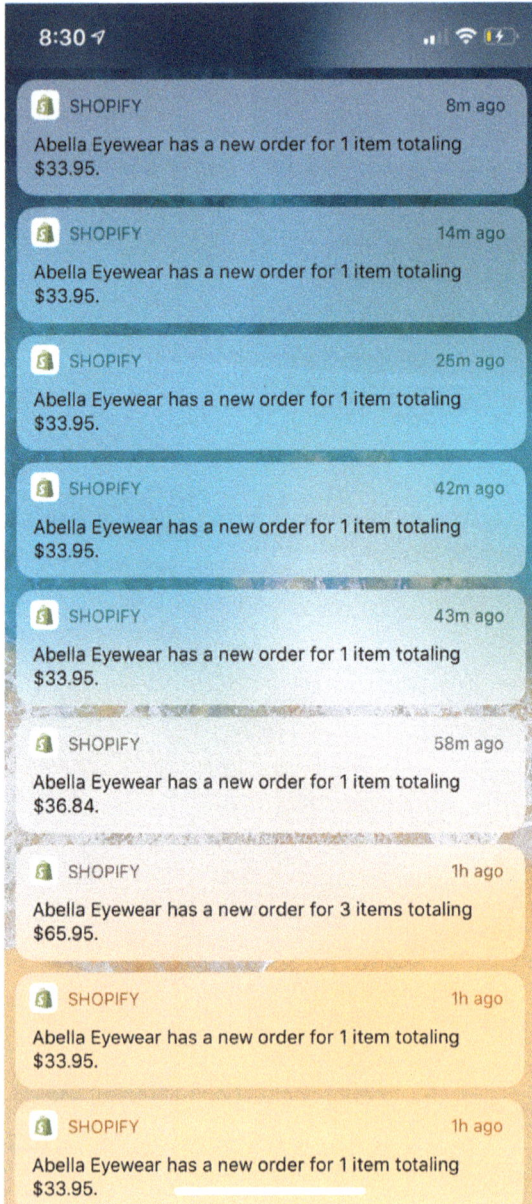

It was working.

And it made sense. Sunglasses didn't have sizing. They didn't require confidence to post in. You didn't need to be half-naked to feel like a brand ambassador. Girls could wear them anywhere, tag us anytime, and still feel like they were part of the movement.

The ad economics were just as good—sometimes better.

And the product was simpler to source, ship, and scale.

We doubled down immediately.

Within days, we were pushing a few thousand dollars a day in sales.

Abella was different.

It was newer money. Bigger money. Faster money.

We weren't just scaling a business.

We were engineering one that could handle scale.

6

Perception Over Product

The product was sunglasses.

Simple. Lightweight. No sizing. No returns.

But now that volume was climbing, we had to make sure what we were shipping actually held up. So we started sampling from factories in China—lots of them. Or at least, we thought they were different factories.

That's when we learned how the game really works.

In China, there's no clean line between factory and broker. Half the time, you're buying from a guy who's buying from the same factory as someone else. You might order two different pairs of sunglasses from two different suppliers, and they end up coming from the exact same line, just with different emails and pricing.

It was a mess.

But it was a revealing mess.

Because what we discovered in the process was simple—

a $5 pair of sunglasses could rival a $350 designer pair.

Seriously. Same materials. Same components. Same build quality.

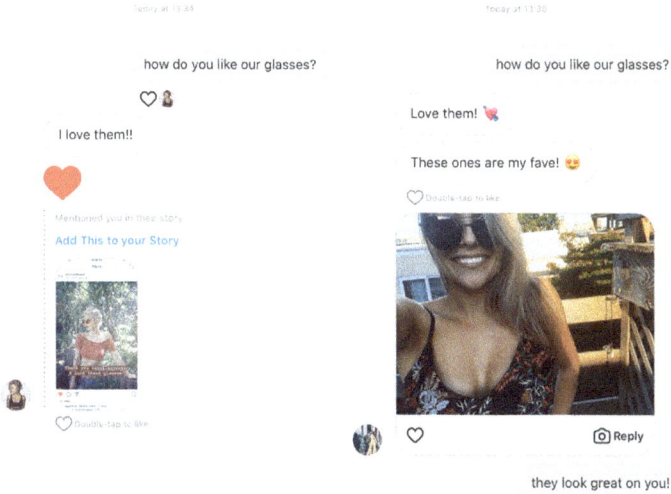

Customer satisfaction was high

We actually looked into the plastics.

Most high-end frames use acetate or polycarbonate—ours did too.

Same hinges. Same bridge components. Same nose pads.

Our Chinese factory had a private showroom in Los Angeles we visited where they dissected the quality of the biggest names in the industry before our eyes.

The materials between our samples and the so-called designer pairs?

Nearly identical.

What set them apart wasn't the construction.

It was the story.

We weren't just guessing, either. Our factory told us the designer pairs we bought from highly reputable stores—to test, tear down, and benchmark—were counterfeit. And not obvious fakes. These were near-perfect matches, indistinguishable from the real thing.

The market was flooded with high-end counterfeits that *matched* the quality of genuine designer frames.

Almost every pair of sunglasses in the world can be made for under $5—regardless of the logo.

So no—it wasn't better product they were selling.

It was better presentation.

Unboxing. Branding. Packaging.

That's where the price lives.

So we leaned in.

We designed our own packaging—heavy boxes with structure and layers. A soft pouch. A branded booklet. Protective inserts.

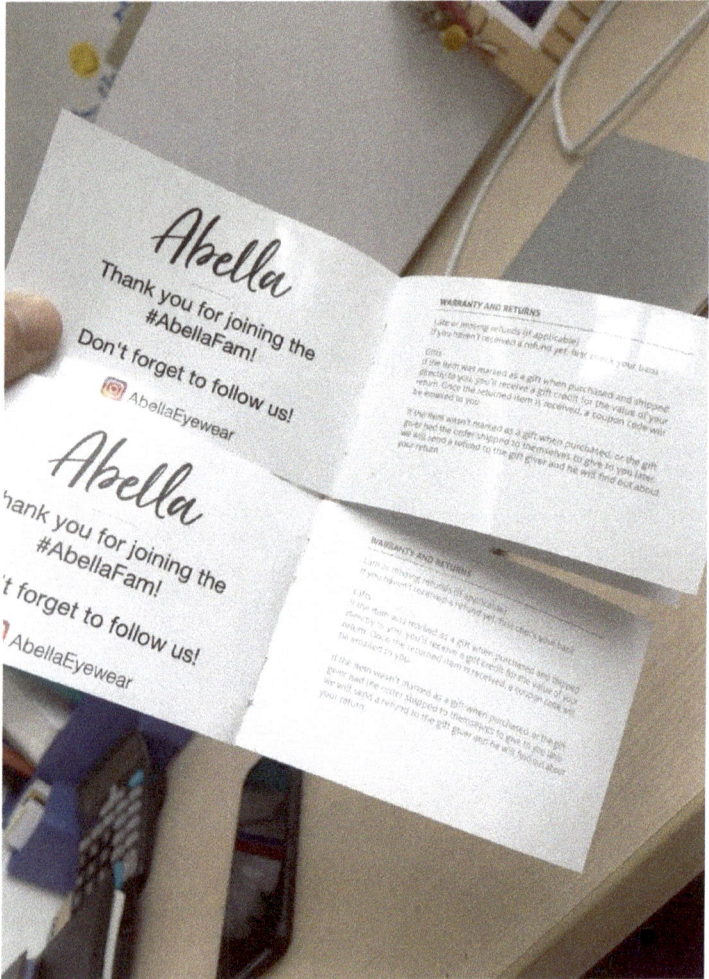

One box even had that slow suction feel when you opened it—like peeling the lid off an Apple product. And that wasn't accidental. Apple's packaging is engineered to let air escape *just* slowly enough to create a pause. It makes you wait. That moment of resistance—right before the lid lifts—is part of the branding.

It tells your brain, *this matters.*

So we borrowed it.

That detail mattered. People noticed. And more importantly, people remembered.

Suddenly, a $5 pair of sunglasses didn't feel cheap.

They felt premium. Aspirational. Giftable.

The product hadn't changed.

But the perception had.

And in this business, that's everything.

There's this strange thing that happens in fashion—where the price tag *becomes* part of the product. A $300 pair of sunglasses doesn't feel expensive because of the materials. It feels expensive because the person holding it knows it costs $300.

Flip the price tags between that and a $20 pair?

Most people couldn't tell the difference.

And even if they guessed right—it would be exactly that. A guess.

Because when two products *look* the same, the value is whatever you're told it is.

We understood that.

By now, we weren't just marketers hacking our way to sales.

We were shaping how people felt about the product.

And that was the turning point.

We weren't selling sunglasses anymore.

We were selling the experience of owning them.

7

Boxes, Warehouses, and a Jeep Full of Money

By this point, sales were strong.

Ad spend was up. Product was dialed. Packaging looked elite.

But behind the scenes, fulfillment was still held together with duct tape and optimism.

We weren't shipping out of our bedrooms anymore. But it had started that way.

Back when we were still doing swimwear, Bryan handled fulfillment from his apartment in California. He used Stamps.com, weighed each package himself, printed the labels, and dropped the shipments outside for pickup. That's how lean we were.

It worked—until it didn't.

One day he messaged me on Skype:

"All the packages are gone."

We figured they'd been stolen. Most likely by a homeless guy walking past the building. And to be fair, he was in California—so the odds were good.

Somewhere out there, a man had just scored a box full of bikinis.

We laughed about it later, but at the time it was pure chaos.

So yeah—getting out of that phase? A big upgrade.

That's when Mason stepped in.

Mason was a connector. A behind-the-scenes operator who seemed to know *everyone*. Need a vendor? A printer? A payments guy? A legal setup in five countries? Mason knew a guy.

He introduced us to a 3PL—third-party logistics—based in Jacksonville, Florida.

They weren't just a warehouse. They were a proper fulfillment partner.

They didn't ship exclusively for us, but just a handful of brands that each had thousands of orders a week.

It was our first real footprint in the physical world.

I happened to be on a road trip through Florida at the time— just me, a girl, and my Jeep, cruising west to east. So we swung through Jacksonville to check it out.

It was surreal.

Truckload of packages headed to customers around the world.

We walked into the warehouse—me, her, and a small entourage of employees showing us around—and saw *our* boxes, *our* product, on racks. In inventory bins. Ready to ship. This wasn't a print-on-demand hustle. This was real inventory, real SKU tracking, real infrastructure. Everything was computerized.

There were many aisles in the warehouse and each aisle had hundreds of boxes like this, each with a unique SKU. Some of these were ours and some were other brands.

I took photos. Sent them back to the team.

None of us had seen it in person before.

But we didn't really need to. Business was smooth.

Still—seeing it *did* something.

I remember two massive cardboard boxes, each easily five feet in every direction, sitting on pallets. Forklift-only territory. No one was lifting those by hand. They were full of inventory— hundreds, maybe thousands of sunglasses packed inside. At the time, we were pushing around a thousand orders a day, so seeing it in bulk like that made sense—but it still hit different.

This wasn't just inventory.

It was *proof*.

What we'd built on screens was sitting here—boxed, labeled, moving.

It wasn't glamorous—but it was legit.

This was the part most people never think about.

The unsexy backend. The actual logistics of making a business work.

But this was also the first time it felt like a company—

Not just a campaign.

8

Stolen Hours, Stolen Dollars

At our peak, we were doing around a thousand orders a day.
Ad spend was climbing. Support tickets were piling up.
Social media mentions, DMs, emails—it was constant.
So we did what any lean team does.
We outsourced.
Support started out simple.
Bryan handled Zendesk. I was asked—tactfully—to stay out of it.
Not because I couldn't manage customers, but because I wasn't built for the script.
I was blunt. Direct. A little *too* real.
To Bryan, it was funny—watching me deliver raw feedback to a customer like we were debating in a group chat.
But customer service doesn't reward honesty.
It rewards tone. Distance. Corporate warmth.
And we were building something bigger than a one-man show.
So Bryan took the lead. And we hired out the rest.
We started with one contractor through Upwork. Then another.

Eventually we had four—full-time, hourly, all based in the Philippines.

They handled every support ticket. Zendesk, DMs, angry emails.

The kind of stuff that would've set us off or derailed our day— They could shrug off without blinking.

And that was the point.

We needed a layer between us and the chaos.

People who could treat customer frustration like another box to check, not a personal attack.

It worked.

Until it didn't.

After several months, something felt off.

Two of them were logging 60+ hours a week, every week. But the work didn't match.

The volume wasn't there. The productivity didn't line up.

And the worst part?

We didn't notice right away—because we were busy closing deals, solving supply chain problems, and pushing ad spend past $7,000 a day.

Eventually, we dug in.

Turned out they were running screen simulators.

Auto-clickers. Tab switchers.

Fake activity designed to trick the Upwork time-tracker into thinking they were working.

And it worked—for a while.

We don't know how much they got us for.

But $20,000 might even be conservative.

Could we have caught it sooner? Yeah.

Should we have had better oversight? Probably.

But would we go back and change it? Honestly—no.

Because at the time, we had bigger priorities.

We weren't short on money.

We were short on *time*.

Every hour we had was going toward ads, creative, inventory, scaling.

Not micromanaging time logs or tracking screen recordings.

The machine was running fast.

And the only thing that mattered was keeping it running.

That's what people miss when they look at businesses like this from the outside.

It's not clean. It's not calm.

It's controlled chaos.

And every once in a while, chaos takes its cut.

9

Scaling Is a Different Business

There's a difference between starting a business and scaling one.

We were learning that in real time.

The creative was working.

The funnel was tight.

Revenue was climbing—$10K days turned into $25K days.

But the mechanics were starting to strain.

We were spending over $7,000 a day on ads.

Inventory orders were ballooning.

Facebook took our money instantly.

Those Patek Philippe watches Mark Zuckerberg wears?

We could've gifted him six and still owed some.

Shopify was taking their cut—and holding onto ours.

That's when Mason stepped in again.

He introduced us to a private payment processor.

Custom rates. Faster settlements. Fewer restrictions.

We'd already upgraded to Shopify Plus, but even that wasn't enough.

At this scale, a 2.9% processing fee wasn't just a cost—it was a tax.

One that stacked higher the faster we moved.

A better processor gave us what we needed:

Cash flow.

Liquidity.

Breathing room.

When you're scaling, time beats margin.

And fast cash is fuel.

We didn't take that extra money and stash it.

We used it.

To buy more inventory.

To test new creatives.

To push spend harder.

That's when we started having the bigger conversation:

What if we had more capital?

The truth is—our third and fourth partners didn't show up at $25K/day.

They came in earlier, right after Abella launched.

We were profitable from day one, but Bryan knew that scaling real volume meant bigger bets.

So he brought in a few serious players.

I didn't know them personally. Still don't.

But I knew what mattered: they had cash, credibility, and the ability to blow this up.

One drove a Ferrari.

Not the post-2020 kind you see in every TikTok reel—this was before the wealth surge, before every crypto kid and ecom coach had one.

Back when it still meant something.

That wasn't the pitch—that was just context.

They were in place before the wave hit.

So when the scale came, we were already strapped in.
This wasn't about raising money to survive.
We didn't need saving.
We were already winning.
But we were building a different kind of company now.
Not just one that could start fast—
One that could *sustain* it.

10

The Burnout Curve

It was inevitable.

No ad angle lasts forever.

We had hit over 25 million impressions in the U.S. alone. Our funnel had run at full blast, day after day, targeting the same core demo: 18 to 24-year-old women. Back then, that market segment was maybe 15 million people total.

We had already passed it.

The numbers started to shift.

Conversion rates slipped. CPMs climbed.

Every customer became more expensive than the last.

Ambassador ads that used to print now limped. Even with constant split testing—new angles, new visuals, new copy—it didn't matter. People had seen it.

And others were copying it.

The ambassador model wasn't a secret anymore. People started copying it—but not at the scale we did it. They weren't running ads. They weren't automating. They were messaging people manually, pitching the ambassador idea one by one, usually over Instagram DMs.

Most of them didn't even have funnels.

No automation. No systems. Just cold DMs and a pitch.

Message, wait, follow up, maybe close a tiny sale. Rinse and repeat.

We didn't panic.

But we weren't blind either.

We were saturating. And not just in theory. It's strange to say out loud—but we were saturating the United States of America. Our ads had touched almost everyone in our target demo.

Even Canada was maxed out.

Pretty sure we hit Australia too, though I can't say for certain.

So we started testing angles for the stragglers—the people who didn't bite on the ambassador pitch.

That's when we launched the quad box.

Same branding. Same quality. New offer.

Buy one pair of sunglasses—get three more free. Four total. Shipped in a custom matte black box with our logo, perfectly molded for four pairs. It was clean. Premium. Giftable.

The quad box.

No one else in the sunglasses space was doing anything like it.

It worked.

I don't know if it beat the ambassador model, but it hit hard.

We brought in big revenue days off it. Another wave. Another reason to keep the engine running.

At the same time, I started looking at wholesale.

I didn't have much experience with it—but the thought was simple: if we're this deep into the market, why not put product on shelves? The trouble was, we had no sales team. No B2B pipeline. Just four partners and a remote support crew. If something needed doing—it was one of us.

So I reached out.

We had decent conversations with a few small retailers, and I think we landed a couple of minor wholesale deals. But nothing massive. No Nordstrom. No Sunglass Hut. Still, it planted a seed.

If retail stores wanted proof—we could give it to them.

We even talked about opening our own storefront. Not for walk-ins. Not for traffic. Just for *social proof.*

If you're spending $7,000 a day on ads and making $20,000 back consistently, then what's $3,000 a month for a physical presence? A real store—maybe something on Ocean Beach in San Diego. An address you could put on the site. A place to film content, tag on Google Maps, and make the brand feel real.

We never pulled the trigger—but it was seriously considered.

Because at this scale, everything becomes about marginal gains.

If a storefront boosted trust—even by a percent or two—that's real money.

That's conversion rate.

That's revenue.

The whole point of this machine was to scale.

We weren't running it for fun.

We were aiming for $100,000 days.

And with four people in the mix, the numbers had to really work. By the time ad spend was paid, inventory was covered, partners were split out—there had to be real profit left on the table.

Not just revenue. Wealth.

Bryan's network wasn't built around small wins. My partners weren't used to running boutique brands. If we weren't getting rich off it—it wasn't worth running.

And that was the new problem.

The funnel still worked, technically.

Orders still came in.
But it wasn't printing anymore.
It wasn't fun.
It wasn't easy.
It wasn't exciting.
The model was burning out.
And the returns were fading with it.

11

The Energy Shift

By this point, we weren't chasing proof of concept.

We had it.

The product worked. The funnel worked. The model worked.

But the momentum? That was fading.

And when you build a business on speed, momentum is the oxygen.

We were out of breath.

Around that same time, Bryan told me he'd taken a big hit in crypto.

It was the tail end of the 2017 bull run, and the market was crashing fast.

He didn't say how much.

Didn't need to.

But I could feel it.

The tone of our conversations shifted.

He wasn't as responsive.

Calls got slower. Less frequent.

We weren't spitballing ideas like we used to.

No urgency. No new hooks. No fire.

There wasn't a formal decision.

No dramatic meeting. No meltdown.

Just a shared sense that this run had peaked.

The ambassador angle was tired.

The team wasn't energized.

The growth wasn't compounding anymore.

And in this game, if you're not compounding—you're dying.

Still, we weren't done throwing punches.

One of our last moves was trying to get onto **Amazon**.

We knew the product was solid. People liked it. The quality held up. But Amazon isn't about quality—it's about trust. And trust on Amazon starts with brand recognition or rock-bottom pricing.

We had neither.

We didn't have a brand people searched for.

No one was typing "Abella" into the search bar.

They were typing "women's sunglasses" and filtering by price.

And when your product is $29.99 and someone else's is $14.99—it doesn't matter how many ad impressions you've run. Most buyers don't care. They don't recognize your brand, and they're not about to pay double for it.

Abella Eyewear Sherwood Metal Frame Polarized Women's Sunglasses

⭐⭐⭐⭐⭐ 1

$29⁹⁵

Ships to Canada

The Abella Eyewear listing on Amazon.

We tried ads on Amazon.

Tweaked the listings. Played with pricing.

But we weren't Amazon guys. We were performance marketers.

We understood front-end funnels, not Amazon FBA.

It wasn't a total flop—some orders trickled in.

Most 20-somethings in that position would have called it a financial success.

But it wasn't scalable.

Not in the way we were used to.

Not in the way that fuels a team used to five-figure days.

And maybe that was the final red flag.

We weren't experimenting anymore.

Some of us were scrambling. Some of us were doing nothing.

Trying to turn a sprint into a marathon—when the model was built to burn hot and fast.

There's a difference between momentum and maintenance.

One builds. The other drags.

And that's where we were—dragging.

12

Time to Cash Out

We didn't announce it.
We didn't post some emotional farewell.
But we knew.
The numbers still made sense on paper—but barely.
The angle was worn out.
The team wasn't excited.
And every day that passed, our upside shrank.
We had built something that *used to* print money.
Now it was just a job.
And that was never the point.
So we decided to sell.
The brand had real value.
Traffic. A customer list. Inventory. Systems.
It was still profitable. Just no longer *worth it*—not for us.
We found a buyer.
No drama. No press release. Just a clean handoff.
And that was that.
Even after the exit, the footprint was still out there.
A year or two later, I met a girl who mentioned she was once

an ambassador for Abella.

She pulled up the emails to prove it.

The brand meant something.

It made it into people's lives—even if only for a minute.

And for something we spun up in five hours on a Skype call?

That's not a bad way to go out.

13

The Angle Was the Asset

People have asked if I miss it.

The brand. The money. The chaos.

Not really.

What we built was fast, fun, and extremely profitable—*for a while.*

But I never confused that with permanence.

It was built on an angle.

And angles get saturated.

That's the difference between most founders and marketers like us.

We didn't fall in love with the product.

We fell in love with the *system.*

The asset wasn't the sunglasses.

It wasn't the Instagram account.

It was the method.

The funnel. The positioning. The offer.

The ability to manufacture demand out of nowhere.

We didn't need startup capital.

We didn't need warm intros.

We didn't even need time.

We needed an idea that burned hot enough to cut through everything else.

That's what *The Ambassador Angle* was.

Not just a tactic.

A playbook.

And when it stopped working—we moved on.

No ego. No mourning. No drag.

That's how real builders operate.

They don't ride a brand into the ground.

They run the angle until it stops printing.

Then they go find another one.

Because once you've done it once—

you know you can do it again.

All we needed was the angle.